The Treasure
that Eyes Cannot See
and other stories

Precious Gift Series

Only a real princess can cry real tears

Nadejda Hristova
Illustrated by Kate and Lilly Aleksovs

The Little Bottle of Tears

Once upon a time in a kingdom far, far away, there lived a princess who was very spoiled. All day long she would cry and insist on having this or that. If she wasn't given what she wanted, she would start weeping inconsolably, "Wa-ah, I want that dress. I want it! I want it!" And her tears would flow like waterfalls down her cheeks.

In vain the king had tried to change his daughter's behavior. Neither pleading with her nor scolding her would bring her to her senses.

One day, an important messenger arrived at the palace. He announced that the prince of a nearby kingdom was looking for a wife and an invitation to a ball was to be given to the princesses of all the neighboring kingdoms. As a sign of his respect, he sent a small gift to each of them. The messenger stepped forward and presented a small golden casket.

The princess looked at the little box and thought to herself, 'I wonder what is inside? It might be a beautiful pearl necklace or sparkling diamond earrings.'

But when she looked inside, she drew back in disappointment. There, nestled on a velvet cradle, was a little empty glass bottle encrusted with golden letters.

"The prince has one condition," the messenger continued. "He will marry the princess who is able to fill the bottle."

"And with what is it to be filled?" the king asked in surprise.

"With tears," the messenger responded, "with the tears of the princess herself."

"Oh, that will be so easy!" the king exclaimed remembering the times the princess had cried countless tears because she could not have what she wanted.

All the courtiers nodded their heads. It was beyond any doubt that shedding tears was what the princess did best.

The arrangements for the ball began immediately. The royal tailors, shoemakers and jewelers worked day and night to prepare an exquisite ensemble for the princess to wear to the ball.

Finally, everything was ready and only a few days remained before the princess would make her journey to the prince's castle. But with all the fuss and ado over what she would wear, the princess had forgotten about the prince's gift.

When she was reminded about the little bottle, she took it from the casket muttering, "Oh, yes, yes! This little bottle needs to be filled with my tears."

The princess immediately opened the bottle, held it to her cheek and began to cry. She wept what seemed like buckets of tears, but when she had finished crying and wiped her eyes, she was amazed to see that the bottle was still empty.

"This is impossible!" She stamped her foot. "What kind of bottle is this?"
She was furious and immediately went to her father.
"This little bottle the prince gave me will not be filled!"

She burst into tears again, but when any of her tears dropped into the bottle, they disappeared at once. The bottom of the bottle absorbed the tears like dry soil drinks up the rain.

The princess was confused. The king was perplexed. Everyone in the palace was mystified. No matter how much the princess cried, none of her tears would remain in the little bottle.

The princess howled and whined continually, "Wa-ah, I want to go to the ball! I want to go to the ball!"

She wailed so much that the king did not have a moment of rest. The king's advisors and the wise men of the kingdom were called to the palace.

"Why not fill the bottle with water," one advised. "No one would ever know."

Another suggested. "Tears are salty, aren't they? We could put some salt in the water."

The princess stopped the chatter, "Never! I will not allow anything but my tears to fill this bottle."

She continued to weep.

With the ball only few days away, the king promised a great reward to anyone who could help his daughter. The news spread quickly throughout the land and many people came to the palace, but all their schemes were futile. Then, just when all hope seemed lost, a woman from a nearby village arrived at the gates of the palace. She was escorted into the presence of the king.

"Your Majesty, I hope I can help your daughter," she addressed the ruler.

"What can be done?" he asked. "Many have tried to help her and failed?"

"Let the princess stay at my home for three days."

The king thought a short holiday for his daughter might be a good thing, but the princess was affronted.

"What? Me? Leave the palace to live in a peasant's house? How dare you make such an offensive suggestion!" she exclaimed indignantly.

The woman replied quietly, "Your Highness, I thought you might be willing to try anything to solve your problem."

She made a bow and turned to leave. As the great doors to the throne room were about to close behind the woman, the princess called out.

"Wait! If I agree, what will I have to do?"

"Put on this dress I've brought for you and follow me," the woman said simply.

The princess looked at the dress the woman held out to her. It was a coarse brown working girl's dress, not the fine pretty silk she was accustomed to wearing. She screwed up her nose and begrudgingly agreed.

"Alright," said the princess proudly tossing her head, "but I'll stay for one day only and not a moment more."

"My condition is that you stay three days, Your Highness" the woman replied calmly.

When they reached the woman's cottage in the village, the princess reluctantly stepped through the front door. The little room prepared for her was clean, but frugally furnished. And the food she was given to eat seemed so tasteless and unpalatable, she could not swallow it.

The hard bed and her empty stomach kept the princess from sleeping all that night. In the morning, she could hear the happy laughter of children through the window. She opened the door of her room to find the woman busy in the kitchen kneading dough for bread. The princess was very thirsty and asked for a glass of water.

The woman nodded. "There is a pail next to the well. My children will help you."

"What? You expect me to…" the princess began resentfully, but fell silent.

The second day was just as difficult for the princess and passed even more slowly than the first. On the third morning, however, she was so desperately hungry that she brought water from the well for the woman and ate a bowl of porridge.

Now the food did not seem so tasteless. The princess also began to help the woman with the household chores and even played with the children in the garden.

As the princess prepared to return to the castle at the end of the third day, the woman spoke quietly to her, "Your Highness, there is no amount of wealth in the whole world that can make you really happy."

Everyone in the palace was looking forward to seeing the king's daughter again. The ball was to be the following day. The king met her in the hope that the peasant woman's plan had worked.

"Well, my child, are you ready to go to the ball?"

She bowed her head. The little bottle she held in her hand was still empty. The princess had spent three days in the peasant's house and during that time she had not wept once. Looking out through the window of the room, it seemed she could still hear the children's happy laughter. They were poor, yet they were content. She lived in luxury with everything she wanted at her beck and call, but she had always been discontent. The woman was right. Each new thing she was given seemed to bring happiness at first, but her heart had remained empty. How her soul longed to find rest.

At that moment, a warm tear fell from her eye.

The small glittering drop rolled down her cheek and fell right into the opening of the little bottle. And, it was a miracle! It did not disappear, but remained there.

The princess no longer wanted to go to the ball. To take the empty bottle now felt more shameful than she had felt going to the peasant's house. But if she didn't go to the ball, the woman would not receive the reward and the princess was truly grateful to her. Reluctantly, she ordered her attendants to prepare her for the ball.

The princess was escorted into the richly decorated ballroom of the prince's palace. Twelve other princesses were already gathered in a semi-circle in the center of the hall. Each was holding a little glass bottle encrusted with golden letters just like hers. And, oh no! All twelve bottles were full.

The princess had the desire to run from the ballroom, but it was too late. The prince was walking towards them. He stood in front of the princesses and bowed.

"Will each of you please show me the present I gave you?" he asked. The prince slowly walked past each princess looking at the bottles with a smile on his face. Approaching the thirteenth princess, he noticed her clenched fist.

"If you don't mind, may I see your present?" he asked gently.

Trying not to show her embarrassment, the princess slowly opened her palm. The prince peered closer. There, at the bottom of her little bottle, the single tear drop glistened. The prince passed her by and then, again standing before them, addressed the princesses.

"I am happy to announce that I have chosen one of you to be my wife."

The excitement of the princesses quickly turned to amazement as he approached the thirteenth princess, knelt before her and asked for her hand in marriage.

"But why did you choose her?" the other princesses cried indignantly with one voice. "Our bottles are full!"

The prince took the little bottle from the hand of the princess and lifted it high.

The encrusted golden letters, of which the princesses had taken little notice, glowed brightly before their eyes as if they were seeing them for the first time.

'Only a real princess can cry real tears,' the letters silently declared.

"All the bottles are the same," the prince explained, "but they cannot be filled within a short period of time. Rather, the whole lifetime of a person is required. And a heart that sincerely yearns for real, worthwhile things. In this little bottle I found only one, but a real tear. That is why I chose her."

At this, the twelve princesses hung their heads because they knew their bottles did not contain tears at all.

The prince looked at the chosen princess and said quietly, "I am so happy to have found you."

And the little bottle collected the princess' tears for the rest of her life.

The Little Bear to Whom Only Good Things Happened

Every morning when the sun smiled behind the crowns of the trees, Little Bear would fetch his school bag and prepare to go to school. He had done his homework diligently and studied his lessons from the day before, but he knew he was not yet ready to leave home. Little Bear would stand before Mother Bear and lift up his head hopefully to her.

"My dear child, may only good things happen to you today," she would whisper to him as she tenderly kissed his little forehead.

"Thanks, Mum," he would answer.

His mother's words made him feel calm and gave him confidence on his journey through the forest to school.

When he arrived at school, his friends were happy to see him.

'My little heart doesn't beat so fast when I'm near him.' Bunny was full of joy at the thought.

'Little Bear is smart and strong,' Little Hedgehog pondered. 'My friends must be just like him.'

Wolfy said to himself, 'Maths is not so difficult when Little Bear helps me.'

Little Snail looked at him with admiration. 'Oh, the world is so different when I can see it from Little Bear's shoulder.'

Little Deer dreamed, 'I want to be like Little Bear.'

Some, however, laughed at Little Bear behind his back and said to each other, "It's so silly to believe that only good things happen to him."

Thankfully, Little Bear never heard these unkind words. He was a happy little bear who thought this day would be filled only with good things.

But one day while on his way home from school, something unexpected happened.

As he was walking through the forest with some of his friends, Little Bear came upon a pile of small branches which covered the path. He had not noticed them earlier in the day when he passed that way going to school.

Suddenly, the branches crackled and snapped under his little feet. He fell down, down, down.

"Help!"

Little Bear's voice faded as he fell into a deep, dark pit which had been freshly dug and carefully covered with the branches. He landed on the soft earth at the bottom of the pit.

Little Bear felt the ground beneath him. 'What happened?' he asked himself. 'Where am I?'

He was thankful he had not been hurt by the fall. He stood up and reached out to feel where he was. The sandy walls of the pit were close. He looked up and saw the light of the sun glinting above the broken branches through which he had fallen.

"Help me!" Little Bear's voice was muffled as he shouted as loud as he could. The sunlight was blocked as heads appeared above. His friends were gathering around the edge of the pit, but no matter how much they peered into the darkness, they could not see Little Bear.

"Little Bear! Little Bear!" The friends' voices seemed so distant, so faint.

"Are you okay, Little Bear?" Little Snail sobbed.

"Little Bear, say something!" Little Deer called.

At last Little Bear responded, "I'm here."

Little Mouse tried to reassure him, "Don't be afraid, my friend. Little Deer will run to get help."

But his voice was so quiet that Little Bear was not able to hear it. Instead of hearing Little Mouse's comforting voice, he heard something he never expected.

"Ha ha ha, only good things happen to him, do they?"

"Ha ha ha, only a fool would believe that. Ha ha ha."

The mocking voices cut through the darkness of the pit.

"Ha ha ha, look Foxy, bad things do happen to Little Bear. Come on Hedgehog, come on Bunny, let's go. There's nothing more for us to do here. Ha ha ha, what fun we've had today."

The laughing voices of Wolfy, Foxy and Little Hedgehog could be heard fading into the distance.

"Oh, my friends, why are you leaving me?" Little Bear sobbed.

At that moment the darkness seemed to engulf Little Bear even more.

"Wait, Mum never lies." Little Bear tried to console himself, but the pit was so cold and dark, his heart grew heavy with sadness. He covered his face with his paws and began to cry.

"Little Bear! Little Bear!" It was Father Bear's voice. "Catch the rope and tie it around your waist. I'll pull you out."

Soon he felt his father's strong paws pulling him up, up into the sunlight. The birds' singing, which a moment before was hushed, now rang out more clearly.

As soon as his feet were set firmly back onto the path he looked up into his father's face.

"Thank you, Dad!"

Father Bear gave him a hug. "My dear Little Bear. I'm so sorry this trouble has come upon you."

"You have wonderful friends," said Mother Bear as she too hugged Little Bear. "It would have been difficult for us to find you without their help."

Little Bear looked at Little Deer, Little Mouse and Little Snail. How happy he was that he could embrace them and say, "Thank you, my dear friends!"

But there was also pain in his heart as he remembered the others who had treated him so unkindly.

'Why did they leave me?' he asked himself as his eyes searched back along the path. 'Did I deceive myself about their friendship? Wolfy, Foxy, where are you? Little Hedgehog, Bunny, don't you know how dear you are to me?'

A short way along the path, Little Bear spotted a small figure huddled in the bushes. He hesitated a moment as he remembered the mocking, laughing voices above the pit.

He then slowly began to smile as he said softly, "Oh that really is him, my own friend."

As he approached, he stretched out his paws to Bunny.

"Forgive me, Little Bear," Bunny sobbed. "I'm so sorry…"

Bunny couldn't continue because of his tears. He couldn't express how, when he had followed the others away, his little feet had become heavier with every step. He couldn't explain how, when standing before Wolfy's large, fearsome teeth, he had remembered Little Bear's friendly smile and that had given him the courage to stop and turn back. And he couldn't describe how fear had filled his little beating heart with dread and had reached to the very tips of his whiskers. It seemed that Little Bear's warm hug buried all of Bunny's explanations, his worries and misdeeds.

Little Bear looked into his friend's eyes. He was ready to do what he never before had the opportunity to experience.

"I forgive you, Bunny," he said quietly and was surprised to feel the pain in his heart slowly melt away.

After Father Bear made a barrier in front of the pit so no one else would fall into it, the Bear family walked the rest of the way together through the forest to their home.

When they had entered their house, Mother Bear spoke gently to Little Bear, "My dear child, I think today was not a day in which only good things happened to you."

"But Mum, the very best thing happened to me today!"

His father smiled. "Um, you found out who your true friends are?"

"No Dad, I can't control how others behave," Little Bear replied, "but it is my responsibility to choose how to respond when my friends come back to me. Today I found out what it means for me to be a true friend."

"And that really is most important," said his father.

His parents smiled and together they hugged their son who was now a much wiser Little Bear.

The Treasure that Eyes Cannot See

In the deep, dark waters of the ocean where the sun's rays barely reach lived the magnificent creatures of the sea. They looked beautiful as they swam around the bottomless depths. Their lives had been calm and carefree, but recently something had begun to trouble them.

The fish gathered together in large schools and were very animated in their debates. The turtles and loggerheads, water mushrooms and corals argued heatedly. The courtiers in the palace discussed the matter all day long. The king of the sea was forced to listen to their conversations from morning until night and wasn't able to assign a single task of work to anyone.

The creatures asked one another the question that was bothering them:

'Who is the most beautiful of us all?'

And this was the subject of their discussions.

One day, having had enough of the nonsense, the king decided to put an end to the argument. On a piece of seaweed the wise ruler wrote:

What is the thing that

Makes you so unique?

Your eyes and face –

Are gifts you can't repeat.

Inside you, what is hidden?

Show it to the king!

Eyes can't see the thing

That you keep within.

And whoever has hidden

A treasure deep inside,

He'll be the first before the king!

The competition is announced!

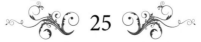

The sea horses, who were the king's heralds, spread the proclamation throughout the kingdom of the sea. All the sea dwellers were invited to the palace and there, each would show what was hidden within them. The winner, chosen by the king himself, could expect a great honour. Indescribable excitement overcame all the creatures.

There was no one more eager to go to the palace than the octopus. He had known for quite some time that his handsome appearance surpassed that of everyone else in the whole kingdom. But now everyone would be astonished at what he had hidden within him.

"What I am filled with inside is so unique. There's nothing more splendid than being able to cover everything around with black ink," he boasted in conceit as he generously spread huge dark clouds all around.

"You are mistaken, neighbor," objected the shark. "It has long been well known that I am the greatest beauty in the kingdom. When what is within me is revealed, there can be little doubt that I am second to none. Nothing is more attractive than my strong teeth. In them true beauty is found."

She smiled, exposing her glistening, sharp teeth arranged in three neat rows.

"Why hide anything at all?" the jellyfish exclaimed. "It is much more effective to be transparent."

She swam about gracefully, folding and unfolding her delicate lacy dress.

"But, my dear friend, then nobody would pay any attention to you," crackled the electric eel. "What is confined within should increase the tension. That is what will make others notice you."

She emitted several electrical rainbows, churning the water around her.

"It would be a big mistake to hide something inside you," the sea-urchin declared. "It is far better to be empty on the inside so you can more easily inflate yourself."

And expanding her belly, she floated about lightly like an enormous balloon.

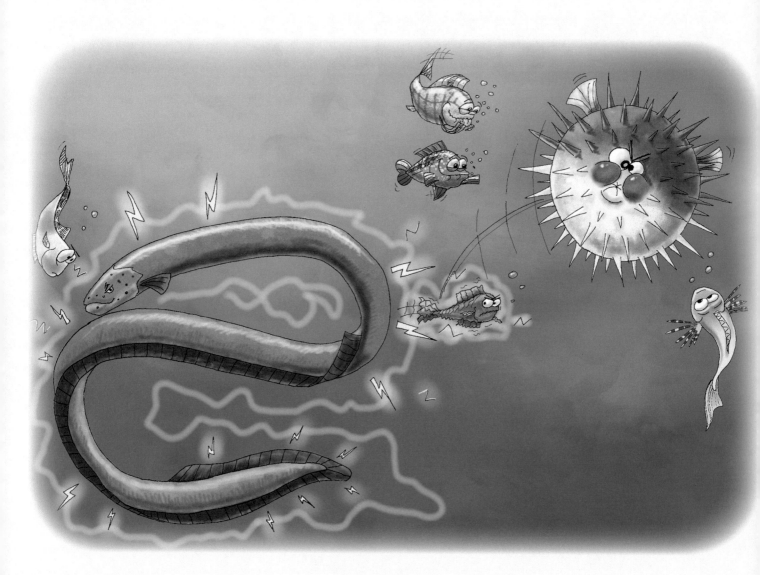

But there was one inhabitant of the sea kingdom who said nothing. She was not proud of her plain appearance and shapeless inside and would never dream of participating in the competition. The little mussel stood in silence on the sea floor and quietly sobbed. Recently, a small grain of sand had lodged itself in her heart and it constantly irritated her, but she had not been able to rid herself of it.

"What's the trouble?" asked the eel. "Don't you like our company?"

The mussel whispered in reply, "Oh, I'm sorry, but it's not what you are thinking. I…"

"Really?" the octopus interrupted. "She probably thinks we are not good enough to see what she has hidden inside."

"No, no, I just…" the mussel tried to explain, but the eel continued.

"You must be very self-confident because you don't even want to speak about it. What are you hiding from us? Show us!"

"Show us! Show us!" the others insisted.

The mussel pressed her little shells together and tried to bury herself in the sand, but the others thought she really was hiding something from them and decided to take her to the king.

"She needs to be taught a good lesson," they said as they took her to the palace.

There, before the astute eyes of the sea ruler, everyone was eager to show what they had hidden inside. The eel was the last creature to show herself and, after lighting up the water around her in a dazzling display, she turned to the king.

"Your Majesty," she crackled, "there is someone else here who considers none of us worthy to see what she has hidden inside. We brought her here to teach her a lesson."

Everyone drew back, leaving the mussel alone under their harsh stares.

"Will you show us what you keep inside hidden from our eyes?" the king asked her kindly.

The mussel trembled. The particle of sand she carried inside her shells would hardly impress anyone, but she need not fear while standing before the king. Slowly, she opened her shells. What a great surprise for all the sea creatures. There, in the very heart of the mussel, glowed a large white pearl.

Her hidden tears had covered the tiny particle of sand with lustrous mother of pearl.

The king stepped forward and took the magnificent pearl.

"And here she is, the winner of our competition," he said waving his hand towards the mussel. "As a reward, from this day on, this pearl will decorate the top of my crown. Thus it will always be a reminder of the most beautiful creature in the whole kingdom."

The sea dwellers were silenced as they made a bow to the king. From that day forward the pearl, which glowed at the top of the crown, silently reminded them of that which eyes cannot see: the exquisite treasure found within a tiny heart.

The Little Sunflower

Little Sunflower opened his little eyes. A light, cool breeze was gently caressing his little face. Behind the outlines of the ridge in the distant, the sun was still hiding.

Little Sunflower could not tell what attracted him to this great ball of warmth and life. He only knew that when the first rays cut through the horizon, he would fix his little eyes on the sun and gaze at it all day long. There was something inexplicable in this, something mysterious: to watch and yearn only for the sun.

His little stem had sprouted and was growing tall and strong at the very end of the sunflower field where he and some other sunflowers surrounded an old walnut tree. A blackbird perched above on one of the tree branches. The bird fixed his eyes on the young head and the sweet, plump seeds of Little Sunflower. How delicious they looked. But the sun was making them dense and sturdy and it would be difficult to detach them from the head. If only the seeds were drier, then they would easily fall into his beak.

The blackbird flitted and perched on a branch closer to Little Sunflower.

"How are you today, my friend?" he greeted Little Sunflower. "It seems to me you don't look very well."

"Why? I feel wonderful," Little Sunflower replied in surprise.

"Well," the blackbird said thoughtfully, "I'm looking at you and wondering why your whole life revolves round the sun. Look at the others, they are happy because they are thinking about themselves. And you think only about the sun. Don't you know its heat and light will wither your delicate skin? And it will deprive you of all your strength."

The blackbird seemed very concerned.

"But what can I do?" Little Sunflower asked gullibly.

The blackbird responded, "You ought to understand that you don't always need the hot sun. After all, you have the shade of this tree to make you feel much better. You should start thinking for yourself."

Little Sunflower shuddered. As sharp as a knife, a thought cut through his slender stem and scorched his core upwards to the yellow leaflets of his crown.

'What if the blackbird is right? Perhaps there is happiness I don't yet know about. Why should I not listen to him? I could live my own life and not constantly follow the sun every day.'

The little sunflower decided to pay attention to the blackbird's advice and try to be more independent. He turned his young head to the trunk of the walnut tree and looked for its dense shade.

He would never have thought the sun could be so insidious, wanting to deprive him of every precious and valuable thing and to take away his very life. He did not dare lift his head to glance at that great fiery ball in the sky. And as each new sun ray streaked across the heavens, his leaflets closed tighter and tighter to protect his tender face from the intense heat.

In vain, the sun extended its warm rays to Little Sunflower. In vain, it looked for its reflection in his little round face. Day after day, Little Sunflower turned his back to the sun and chose the shade of the walnut tree.

One day, a yellow butterfly approached Little Sunflower. She could remember his gentle scent which always reminded her of the aroma of a warm sun: the air filled with the fragrances of summer. It had always invigorated her soul and she longed to again be refreshed. But the moment Little Sunflower spotted her, he closed his petals even more tightly.

"My dear Little Sunflower, I have come to see you. Why won't you look at me, Little Sunflower?" the butterfly asked in alarm.

"Don't bother me! Leave me alone!" Little Sunflower turned his head away.

At these words, the butterfly's little heart was filled with a stabbing pain and felt as if her winglets had been broken. She was gasping for air and did not have the energy to fly away.

She needed to recover and with little strength remaining, struggled to a nearby branch and rested.

The butterfly started to weep, "Why doesn't he want me? How have I hurt him? Why is he hiding from me?"

One by one her tears fell onto her wings.

'But I must not cry,' the little butterfly sobbed to herself. 'It will be impossible for me to fly with wet wings.'

She heard a familiar voice.

"Little Sunflower has not been offended by you," said the walnut tree rustling its leaves. "The color of your wings reminds him of the one he no longer wishes to see. That is the reason he does not want to see you."

"Who is he avoiding?" the butterfly asked, raising her little head.

"The sun. Someone convinced him that the sun is his enemy."

The little butterfly was perplexed, "But who would do that?"

"Who do you think?" whispered the walnut tree. "It was someone who would benefit the most: the blackbird!"

"But why didn't you stop him? Why didn't you help Little Sunflower?"

"He would not listen to me. See how tightly closed his petals are. See how he struggles. Since he believed the blackbird's lies, everything within his heart has gone wrong. Now he doesn't know who to trust. He even thinks his friends are enemies."

"We must help him!" the little butterfly lowered her wings. Her tears had made them so heavy.

"We can help him only if he will let us," the walnut tree said quietly.

The little butterfly bowed her little head and sighed.

'My poor Little Sunflower,' she thought, 'now the world is a frightening place for him. The sunlight does not give him any joy; it terrifies him. Even the color of my wings fills him with dread.'

Now her love for Little Sunflower was even deeper. She knew he had never hidden himself from anything before. He had always greeted each morning with such joy. He eagerly awaited the little flying creatures who frequently visited him. The little butterfly was sure he was now unhappy.

And she was right. Never before had Little Sunflower suffered so much. There was something different in the heart of his stem. It was thin and fragile with an emptiness that was big and hollow. He had little strength left to tighten his withering leaflets. There was no desire within him to fight. He hopelessly hung his little head low to the ground.

The butterfly spread her wings.

"Little Sunflower, listen to me, you cannot live without the sun! Do you not know you are its namesake?" She continued to hover around him. "You even look like a little golden sun."

Little Sunflower slowly lifted his drooping head. But he dared not look to the sun from which shafts of light were brightly radiating down to the earth.

A single ray penetrated the dense shade of the walnut leaves searching for Little Sunflower. It tenderly caressed his faded leaflets. Warmth slowly began to fill his withered body, but he was still not able to lift his face and look at the sun. He had believed those terrible lies and now had so little strength.

43

The sun continued looking for his face as if whispering: 'Look to me, look to me.'

Finally, little by little, the sunflower's strength returned. He lifted his face and eagerly focussed on the sun which seemed to be standing still, high in the sky, waiting patiently for the gaze of those two little eyes.

And Little Sunflower smiled. Happiness was returning to warm his heart. His sturdy stem stood upright. His head was now upturned and his yellow leaflets fully opened facing the light. Never again would he turn his back to the sun. Never again would he hide from it. Instead, he would declare:

"I am a SUN-flower with a face that desires only to watch the sun."

Acknowledgements

I would like to extend my utmost appreciation to those who have helped turn this book into the quality product it has become – the translators of the original Bulgarian texts: Galina Dobreva and Emilia Handzhiyska; the editor of the English texts and her tremendous help: Marcia Patterson; the graphic designer: Rossen Antov; Diana Smilenova, a teacher who dreamed of seeing this series of books reach children throughout the world; the illustrators: Kate and Lilly Alexovs without whose eagerness this project would not have been possible. I also thank my husband who never ceased to encourage me. And last, but not least, I thank God who has always inspired me.

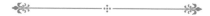

WestBow Press books may be ordered through booksellers or by contacting:

WestBow Press
A Division of Thomas Nelson & Zondervan
1663 Liberty Drive
Bloomington, IN 47403
www.westbowpress.com
1 (866) 928-1240

Because of the dynamic nature of the Internet, any web addresses or links contained in this book may have changed since publication and may no longer be valid. The views expressed in this work are solely those of the author and do not necessarily reflect the views of the publisher, and the publisher hereby disclaims any responsibility for them.

Cover illustration by Kate Aleksova.
Interior illustrations by Kate Aleksova and Lilly Aleksova.

ISBN: 978-1-5127-0999-5 (sc)
ISBN: 978-1-5127-1000-7 (e)

Library of Congress Control Number: 2015914008

Print information available on the last page.

WestBow Press rev. date: 10/16/2015

WESTBOW
PRESS®
A DIVISION OF THOMAS NELSON
& ZONDERVAN

Printed in the United States
By Bookmasters